The De

ABOUT THE AUTHOR

Snail is thought to have been born in 2003, in a hedge in Scarborough, North Yorkshire, where he lived until his death in 2009.

ABOUT THE TRANSLATOR

Jamie McGarry was born in Norwich in 1988, and grew up in North Wales and East Yorkshire. He attended university in Scarborough, earning a degree in English Literature and Culture, and in 2008 he founded independent publishing house Valley Press, which he continues to run to this day. After uncovering and translating the original 'snail diary' in 2009, Jamie made it his mission in life to honour the author's memory and spread the word of his literary prowess far and wide.

A slow-moving, brown-hued creature, Jamie regularly enjoys a leafy salad, and has (on occasion) been known to come out of his shell.

ABOUT THE ILLUSTRATOR

Emma Wright studied Classics at Oxford and worked in ebook production at Orion Publishing Group before leaving to set up The Emma Press in 2012. She first read *The Dead Snail Diaries* on her poetry book stall in Lower Marsh Market and was gripped by the desire to publish it.

Also from The Emma Press:

The Emma Press Anthology of Mildly Erotic Verse
A Poetic Primer for Love and Seduction: Naso was my Tutor
The Emma Press Anthology of Motherhood
The Emma Press Anthology of Fatherhood
Homesickness and Exile (Sept 2014)
Best Friends Forever (Dec 2014)

The Emma Press Picks:

The Flower and the Plough, by Rachel Piercey
The Emmores, by Richard O'Brien
The Held and the Lost, by Kristen Roberts
Captain Love and the Five Joaquins, by John Clegg

Pamphlets:

Ikhda, by Ikhda, by Ikhda Ayuning Maharsi
Raspberries for the Ferry, by Andrew Wynn Owen
Rivers Wanted, by Rachel Piercey (Oct 2014)
Oils, by Stephen Sexton (Oct 2014)
Myrtle, by Ruth Wiggins (Nov 2014)
If I Lay on my Back I Saw Nothing but Naked Women,
    by Jacqueline Saphra (Nov 2014)

The Dead Snail Diaries

by Jamie McGarry

for everyone
who feels
not quite far enough
from the ground

THE EMMA PRESS

First published in 2011 by Valley Press
This edition first publishing in 2014 by The Emma Press Ltd

Text copyright © Jamie McGarry 2014
Illustrations copyright © Emma Wright 2014

ISBN 978 0 9574596 9 4

A CIP catalogue record of this book
is available from the British Library.

Printed and bound in Great Britain
by Jasprint, Washington.

theemmapress.com
editor@theemmapress.com

Contents

Introduction

Have you ever stepped on a snail? Not on purpose, of course – I know you would never do such a thing – but by accident, perhaps when hurrying home along a dark, rain-slick street.

I have. It was back in May 2009, and – as was the style at the time – I recorded the incident and my subsequent guilt in a poem titled 'The Haunting of Poet by Snail'. After finishing this piece, I felt somewhat better about things; enough that I could face returning to the scene of the crime, which my long-suffering therapist assured me was an essential step in putting the incident to rest.

When I arrived at the spot, I found several things I did not expect. First, the body had been moved; just a chalk outline remained, indicating the final pose and position of the victim. (Exactly who might have drawn this remains a mystery – I think I also saw a tiny piece of police tape cordoning off the area; but my memory may be playing tricks.) The more important discovery, off to one side behind a tuft of grass, was a very small red book. I knew it could only be one thing: the dead snail's diary, presumably thrown aside during the carnage that fateful night.

The contents were written in a mysterious language, which I now know as Modern Snailish. I immediately set to work producing a translation, and was stunned to discover that I had crushed a writer of some ambition and literary talent. The diary contained details of the snail's day-to-day life and his role in an astonishingly complex society of minibeasts, acted out just a metre or two below ours. Even more remarkably, I found familiar works of human literature altered (sometimes drastically) to suit an audience of snails, and an entirely new seafaring adventure that may or may not have been the snail's first attempt at a verse novel.

I knew what I had to do: write up the contents of the diary in English, maintaining the snail's original form (usually poetic) wherever possible, and distribute it as widely as I could, so that humanity might better understand our slimy, shell-dwelling neighbours. After years of struggling alone, I have finally found a willing partner in this effort – The Emma Press – whose publisher believes my story wholeheartedly, and has even gone to the effort of reproducing the snail's humble attempts at illustration.

The snail's life may have ended on that dark, rainy night, but his story did not. I hope you enjoy this book, and do please try to read it at a slow and steady pace; I feel sure that's what he would have wanted.

J.M.
August 2013

The Dead Snail Diaries

The Haunting of Poet by Snail

Has it been four days now?
Must have been. Nearly a week
since I did the deed. It was dark,
and I was hurrying – I didn't see
his form, the path in front of me.
My careless size-ten shoe came down,
and crushed his hopes and dreams.

My stride stopped mid-step. Sickened
by that sound, the chilling crunch;
I saw him, when I lifted up.
A tragic mix of slime and shrapnel.

And now – although you'll doubt –
I swear he's back. I am the mollusc's
sole unfinished business
on this fast and brutal Earth.

You'll say it's in my head, if I report
I can hear his death
in every mistimed gearshift,
every mouth devouring crisps.

But it's not my conscience doing this,
it's *him*. He's putting me through hell.
I hear, with every step I take,
the breaking of the tell-tale shell.

Last night, I thought I saw him,
bright and cold, in death,
slowly sliding next to me;
I felt his tiny, ghostly breath.

'It was dark!' I scream. 'I was hurrying!'
His silence says it all. But still,
you don't believe me? Come on round,
see the trails across my walls...

and explain the vengeful holes
in my fridge-ridden, cellophaned lettuce.

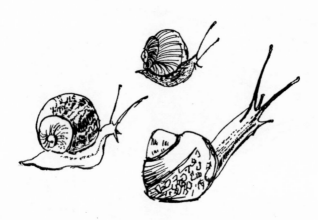

A Love Poem: From Snail to Slug

God made us brown so we'd be hard
to spot upon his fertile soil;
to hide from the birds (which he made as well),
to cower, dodge, to postpone hell.

But slug does not hide, or flinch back.
His coat? Uncompromising BLACK.
He turns defence into attack.
Oh slug – oh glorious slug.

God gave us shells to weigh us down.
Without them, we would HURTLE round,
so common sense suggests. Who'd beat us,
across a distance of ten metres?

But slug, dear slug, you have the grace
to not rub freedom in our face;
you slow your stride to match our pace.
Oh slug – oh glorious slug.

God made us quiet, thoughtful, wait.
He taught us manners, and restraint.
He taught us not to stay out late,
we're model garden citizens.

But slug, he DEAFENS when he speaks!
He goes out seven nights a week!
Beer-swilling, hard-living, party beast.
Oh slug – oh glorious slug.

I'd sell my soul to be like him.
Vacate my shell, and dye my skin.
I'd go twice weekly to the gym,
if doing so would let me in

to doors in town that say 'slugs only'.
But slug accepts no fake, no phony.
I'll love, but I will never be
a slug – oh glorious slug.

Slug's Night Out

It starts with getting all done up –
in black, of course. Straighten the antennae.
Then off, for the usual night on the tiles,
on the Johnsons' fresh-laid patio.

We're the cool kids round here. Tough as luck.
'Ain't no insect gonna mess with us!'
When the rest are tucked up in their beds,
we rule this town. Back door to fence.

Some call us anti-social. (The Johnsons?)
They deride our slime-art. Describe it in
their high society, garden magazines
as 'disgusting, unsightly, abhorrent'.

They wouldn't know life if it bit them in the face.

Snails? Those garden geeks? That's rich.
They don't have half the charm we have.
I could take them any day, cool as.
Front end tied behind my back.

We don't touch the pellets – the hard stuff.
Salt. We're tough, but we ain't mad.
But we're all on the grass, and I once had this mate,
nibbled his way through a catnip plant.

We lost one last night, drowned himself
in a vat of lukewarm beer. It's sad,
but there's worse ways to bow out. My mother
warned us that we'd wind up dead...

But we'll all be dried up in the end,
so excuse us if we live till then.

The Snail Not Taken

after Robert Frost

Two snails diverged on a plank of wood;
it's not clear what they're parting for.
Some careless words, misunderstood,
have come between these souls; once good
but now approaching all-out war.

There's some dispute, about a leaf.
First claimed by one, and then the next.
Each so secure in their belief
that the other should be called the thief,
the debate has lost all context.

Now, they race to split apart,
to get some distance from their foe.
Clearly, it was that, or start
to tear the other one apart;
I thought it best to help them go.

I plucked one from the right-hand side,
and placed it carefully on a fence.
Two snails diverged on wood, and I,
I moved the one with regret in its eyes –
and hoped it would make a difference.

Diary of a Church Snail

after John Betjeman

Down here among the crimson robes
choir boys (and girls) wear, over clothes,
there's a lunch-box that's no longer full,
and slime on '... bright and beautiful,
all creatures great and small.' That's me.
At home in either category
(although I'm not a 'snail of cloth',
or affiliated with a god).
I'm not here for the food – that's clear –
those hymn books give me diarrhoea,
and as for bread and jam, they're worse.
(Why don't mankind bring veg to church?)
I know what you are thinking, all,
'At least there's Harvest Festival',
but by the time *I'm* there, the vicar's
tidied up ahead of Christmas.

So why, you ask, am I still here?
A vestry-dweller, year on year?
Living off the dying flowers
the ladies drop by after-hours,
instead of carving out a gash
across the vicar's cabbage patch?
Well, I find it's camouflaging,
hiding out among the carving –
my humble shell is rather good
at fitting in with sculpted wood.
Also, though perhaps surprising,
I find that I agree with Larkin:
though empty, obsolete, and cold
this place does wonders for my soul.

8

It used to be the case, at Christmas,
there'd be some extra visitors:
earthworms, centipedes, woodlice
(and even those too-smug church mice).
While I live here the whole year round
they'd only creep out of the ground
the once; towards the end of year
to grab themselves some Christmas cheer.
And now, not even that. Just me
and Reverend turn up regularly;
though he may well give up for good
once I lie static on the wood.
Drop by and see us – bring some flowers,
bring comfort to these Christian hours,
and note, though cold and thin, I stay;
when all the rest have run away.

The Hollow Snails

after T.S. Eliot

I.

We are the hollow snails.
We are the dead snails.
Our voices, now echoing wind
through empty shells. Alas!
No-one lays wreaths
made of the blooms
we loved in life,
now we lie dead upon the grass.

They say we have the look
of jamless jar, of pageless book.
Shape without motion; protection
without life to protect. Remember us –
if at all – not as gaping holes,
not as spent vessels of good souls,
but only as the hollow snails.
The dead snails.

II.

We are the crushed snails.
We are the squashed snails.
Trampled underfoot,
by thoughtless poets
(such as Eliot).

We will live on in your dreams,
snails as tall as trees –
eyes on stalks, swinging
eyes you dare not meet.

You will hear our voices in the wind,
you will remember
our first, and final encounter,

the damp patch on the patio
glinting in the sunlight
like a fading star.

III.

We are the smashed snails.
We are the shattered snails.

Plucked from the prickly pear
at five o'clock in the morning,
carried and dropped by gulls

from a great height.

We fell. We were dead,
but for a second
between existence
and our end
we cast a shadow

from a height.

You saw us
from a window,
between release
and our demise

from a great height.

Between the motion
and the vision,
between death
and our descent
we cast a shadow

from a great height

on your heart

from a height.

Not with a whimper but a bang.
Not with a whimper but a bang.

Snail Browner Than Ever

after Ted Hughes

Some species, I swear,
were made to suffer.

Noah didn't want them on the ark.
They tried to sneak on board one night,
but he saw their slime, the moonlit shine,
and threw them back into the dark.

They learned to swim –
which isn't easy,
when you've only got one foot.

They don't remember Eden,
HE doesn't remember THEM.
They must have come from somewhere,
but how, and where, and when...

They tried to give sweet Mary
a ride to Bethlehem!
They got themselves assembled, but
he'd been crucified by then.

And now, millennia later,
their rejection is complete.
The world grows ever upwards,
without glancing at its feet,

at the snails, still down there,
browner than ever –

flying their slippery flag
of surrender.

Snail Goes Speed Dating

'The garden snail's courtship dance can last anywhere
from two to twelve hours [...] it concludes with the snails
firing a calcified 'love dart' at their partners, a kind of tiny
Cupid's arrow.'

– Wikipedia, 'Land snails', circa 2010

Love does not move quickly.
Not for snails. Our pace is glacial.
Even mutual love at first sight
cannot be consummated
for several minutes, till
we slide into close contact.

'They rushed into each other's arms...'
Not quite. While aiming to collide
most snails exhaust all conversation,
find out each other's affectations,
become a bit resentful, even –
and when they reach a mating distance
just glare and slide right by.

A single red rose is a buffet.
A daisy? Eaten on the way.
Snail dating is an uphill climb,
snail dating is a loser's game,
so imagine, if you please, how poorly
we fare now they've added 'speed' to the name.

Slug, though, somehow's always great.
He smirked when I asked for his secret
(since in truth, I *do* want a mate...)
'Snaily, dude, no worries!
You'll have noticed how we're pushed for time?'
(I had. I'd struggled to reach one
before the buzzer moved us on.)
'My secret comes in stunning rhyme,
with *pre-perfected chat-up lines.*'

I didn't look convinced. 'Just listen.
These lines will make your mate's skin glisten.'

Hey baby. Want to win my heart?
Come here and calcify my dart...

I'm your Prince Charming, Cinderella.
Let's tangle up our four antennae...

Let's cross our gleaming paths of slime,
along the short path back to mine...

'A little *blue*, Slug.' 'There's no harm in
having fun! They find it charming!'
He winked. 'You'll see. Before the morrow,
under the Johnsons' new wheelbarrow –'
'That's quite enough.' '– ol' Slug
will have been struck with Cupid's arrow.'

Ugh. What is it that he's eating?
I can't work out these foolish snails
who have a deep-set love of slugs,
who hanker after shell-less tails.
Snail dating's tricky just with us,
without competing with the slugs.
Snail dating's hopeless, doomed to crack
if slug-kind hoovers up the pack.

Another thing: you can't rely
on who's a gal and who's a guy.
My first 'speed date' looked like success
till I went to compliment her dress
and found she'd somehow changed her sex –
HE barked at me in bass tones: 'NEXT!'
Oh, molluscs. What did I expect?

I slithered home alone that night.
No 'ticks'. A garden pest.

I dodged the slug's pre-claimed wheelbarrow,
and in the process, drowned my sorrows
with a shortcut through the garden pond,
and thought how best I might respond.

Floating upside down in murk
I watched my dark reflection,
a sad and wonky echo, till
the gloom began to lessen...

I saw flowers, eaten, at a wedding.
My lover, met in one chance meeting,
my children, bright and shiny-shelled –
with eyes on stalks, this snail beheld
what must have been the perfect course,
all love, no chaos or divorce;
the details of a happy future
in a mirror held above the water.

I spun the right-way up, broke through
the shining surface of the pond,
but found the things I saw there, gone.
And cried for I remained, still, one.

But later, in cold morning light
I thought that what I saw was life,
the opportunities still mine,
if I could only realise
that love, like all things grand, takes *time* –

and that, at least, I have
in great supply.

A Snail's Advice to His Son

after Gervase Phinn

Always keep your shell clean, son.
It shows the world you care.
Hold your antennae straight and proud
and pointing in the air.

Trail your slime in crisp, clean lines
in parallel to walls,
stick to grass where dogs are banned
(and games involving balls).

If you must steal mankind's veg
wait till they're not around.
Steer well clear of allotments ('least
until the sun's gone down).

Although you may not have one, son,
be sure to chance your arm.
Confronted by a gang of slugs,
let your response be calm.

Keep your head in times of stress
(inside your shell, if poss).
When I am gone, just carry on.
Smile, despite your loss.

Keep that sense of patience,
never let your stride be rushed;
and don't take life too seriously, son,
for few survive uncrushed.

Pringleplanks: The Railway Snail

from 'Old Possum's Book of Sensible Snails', 1937

There's a holler most irate, at 11:38
when the Snail Mail's ready to up anchor,
saying 'Pringle, where is Pringle, *is he flirting with a thimble?*
We're screwed without that slimy little chancer!'
All the guards and the commuters and the Ticket-Max
    computers
search for him online and, well, on line
crying 'Pringle, where is Pringle? He's the one and only thing'll
stop the nation's post from leaving here on time!'
By 11:43 those involved (hysterically)
start to root through luggage for their mollusc mascot.
Then Pringle will resurface, just in time to start his service
wearing an expression that says: '... what?'
    Then he gives one wave of his tiny prongs
      and the signal flicks to green,
    and we're off at last (though not all *that* fast)
      for what's North of Aberdeen.

You'll be shocked to understand that a snail is in command
of the train that runs this vital night-time route,
but relax, it's all been planned – Pringle has the job in hand
(and besides, you must admit he's rather cute).
While there are those who disparage, claim he can't traverse
one carriage
in the time it takes from King's Cross up to Glasgow,
they've got their wires crossed – Pringle's job is keeping watch;
eyes frontwards, focused on the track below.
Should you venture down to meet him, he will nod a quiet
greeting,
but turn, as always, to his crucial role.
Never take the snail for granted – he's figurehead, a standard;
he signals when you've passed Hadrian's Wall.
   'This is the Night Snail, crossing the border!'
     Pringle seems to say
    (but we've no time for poor old Auden,
      only one spoof poem today).

Now the journey's halfway done, you can almost see the sun
rising somewhere to the East of Holy Island,
and though you'll hear an 'Ahh' running up and down your car,
the snail that saw it first will keep his silence.
His fellow train employees like to see him and swap stories,
and agree that Pringle helps to start their day;
when they board at Edinburgh, the new shift's delight is
    thorough
and the shout with which they greet him is 'HOORAY!'
In fact, he's so revered that, not only is he cheered,
they've given him a share of company stock,
and at Christmas (though ridiculous, for tradesmen so
    meticulous)
they're known to let young Pringle run the signal box.
    But if you return to your cosy seat,
      and think this all seems insane –
    you ought to reflect, upon passing each station,
    that you are protected from most vegetation;
    there's no-one so fine spotting leaves on the line
      as the *Snail of the Railway Train*!

All he needs when feeling peckish is a tiny piece of lettuce
and a shot-glass full of water lasts all night,
though a teaspoon of mild beer keeps the lookout in good
cheer
(provide that, and you'll have a friend for life).
You were sleeping outside York, and so you never thought
that a snail had warned the driver of a cow;
but the pilots all know Pringle, and have learnt his set of
signals,
that him waving his antennae means 'SLOW DOWN!'
When you reach your destination, out upon the final station
you'll see Pringle, standing solo with a smile.
You should give a nod of thanks – for you rode a thousand
tracks,
and it's Pringleplanks who helped you all the while.

Then he stands, at the front of his slimy trail,
waving feelers once again;
saying: 'Now you know who put the "snail" into "mail" –
'twas the *Snail of the Railway Train*.'

Einstein's Snail

Einstein had a theory
that when travelling at speed,
time would pass much faster
than it seemed –

while for those who travel slowly
it would still feel very long,
and he had a snail to tell him
he weren't wrong.

In Search of the
Great Green Sea Snail

ONE: CAPTAIN MAX (FORMERLY PHIL)

Your oft-praised human goals
will be the end of all of us;
man and beast, snail and slug,
one day you'll surely screw it up.

I knew a human once, thought great,
was with him when he met his fate,
and now I come to tell the tale –
like Moby Dick, except with snails.

Maximus, he called himself
(though one day, hidden on a shelf
I found a copy of his will –
turns out his name was really Phil).

His mission, now passed into myth,
was track down (if it did exist)
the Great Green Sea Snail, ancient song
suggests could be a half-mile long,

and ship it back to England. He'd
drag it, caged, to Sotheby's;
and if no-one should make the purchase
he'd sell it to the French, for burgers.

And me – just for the sake of speed –
he found me chewing on a leaf,
and as I wasn't properly stuck
he took me on the trip. For luck.

TWO: ACROSS THE SEA

The ship was cheered, the harbour cleared,
the day the *Treader* disappeared
in densest fog, which choked the air;
Max didn't spot the omen there.

I found life on that ghastly cruiser
ugly (well, at least the crew were).
A reluctant crewman, I suspected
most were coastguards who'd defected,

or just pirates, who'd decided
they no longer got excited
at the prospect of more looting;
so had switched to mollusc shooting.

I tried to keep well out of sight
when Max doled out the rum at night,
in fear they'd number my six sides
and use me as a makeshift die;

I tried to hide out in the day
in case they hooked me up as bait
(as fish just off the coast of Wales
are deeply fond of juicy snails).

Frankly, I was most aggrieved
at having been brought out to sea,
and shouted (though outside their hearing)
'I don't remember volunteering!'

I tried to raise this with the Captain
but he was far too busy laughing,
full of glee at what he'd do
once his prize snail slid into view.

I became still more enflamed with woe
when Max picked up his wife's crossbow
she'd given him for luck, and shot
a cheery passing albatross –

I paced the deck (as best I could)
convinced this portent was not good;
Max and his crew ignored my hunch,
and had the tross's wings for lunch.

After weeks of sailing senseless,
the crew were fast becoming restless,
suspecting that the Great Green Snail
was just a strangely-shapen whale,

when the lad up in the sparrow's nest
flapped as if he'd been possessed,
waving westwards with both hands
crying out 'IT'S LAND, SIR, LAND!'

The Captain was extremely pleased
so (having packed his eight CDs)
he left the crew to dice and fishing,
and took me on an expedition.

A desert island's what we found,
standard issue – sandy, round.
An island which, if asked, I'd say
had been attacked with PVA.

'This isn't glue,' said canny Max,
'There's only one beast makes these tracks,
we're literally ON the trail
of the legendary *Great Green Snail*!'

We left the island then, forthwith,
and once returned on board the ship,
Max stationed me to starboard side
at water's edge, to see if I

could hear the sea-snail's famous song.
(It seems I had been brought along
not for luck, or cunning strength
but hope our waves were similar length.)

The crew looked on all through that day
while I thought of what best to say,
and how to say it – a form of speaking
that could dissuade a human being –

when I heard the sweetest string of notes,
a vocal, bass, to soothe the soul,
and saw below me, 'midst the brine,
a shape that looked a lot like mine.

I knew at once it would be cruel
to lead these men to nature's jewel,
so shouted at that emerald shape:
'THEY MEAN YOU HARM! YOU MUST ESCAPE!'

But she could not quite hear my shout,
so swam on up to check it out –
the Great Green Sea Snail pierced the surface.
My fault! My traitorous disservice!

The sudden sight had shocked the crew
who stood, slack-jawed, without a clue;
eye-contact with their Great Green prey
had taken their resolve away.

'Do something!' shouted Max, until
the cabin boy (with zero skill
in shooting *or* in life) did shiver,
and caught his finger on the trigger.

The hot lead pinged off Great Green's shell,
a slight she seemed to take quite well –
or would have done, if Max's crew
had not all blindly followed suit.

The volley of ballistics seemed
to wake the Sea Snail from her dream,
through narrowed eyes our victim peered
and then – in seconds – disappeared.

'We've lost her!' Max exclaimed. Not true.
We felt the ship begin to move,
the water round our borders swirled,
while seamen screamed like little girls...

I hurried up the starboard side,
confounded by the darkened sky
and growing winds, and sudden rain –
a change I still cannot explain.

The ship was carried far off course,
by winds that fate had made gale force;
we hid below-decks, rode it out,
kept all the hatches battened down.

By now, my general consternation
at being in this situation
had turned to outright rage. Alas,
I couldn't take it out on Max –

I couldn't tell him how I felt
about the hand that he had dealt
this garden creature; human speech
remained beyond my humble reach.

One day the storm-front finally died,
so Max and co. stepped out, to find
on decks where they'd once strolled with ease,
they couldn't feel the slightest breeze.

Stranded, now. Becalmed. Of course,
not only were we far off course,
they'd used all petrol in the storm
to keep their sea-pyjamas warm.

But Max refused to back down now.
'I bet the Sea Snail's still around!
If I know her malicious mind
she'll stick around to watch us die.'

So underneath both sun and moon
the crew stood poised with their harpoon
singing out – the criminals –
'If I could talk to the animals...'

But days turned into weeks, and still
the water lay completely still,
while Max (with admirable will)
stayed focused, ready for the kill.

The crew were looking somewhat glum,
not least since they'd run out of rum:
they'd water, but no drop to drink;
they'd gin, but hadn't brought the tonic.

I slept through all this consternation,
and caught up on some hibernation –
but woke from my much-needed sleep
on sensing tremors from the deep.

The crew thought their despair was over.
'We'll soon be safely back in Dover!'
Convinced the ship's renewed momentum
was from a breeze that God had sent 'em.

I tried a warning – but, too late.
No longer satisfied to wait,
the Sea Snail burst out from the blue,
and smashed the *Treader* clean in two.

'Don't panic!' cried the Captain. 'We
need not fall dead into the sea!
We still can make the homeward trip
so long as we have half a ship!'

SMASH! The Snail emerged again,
and cleft the ship's two halves in twain,
at which Max re-affirmed his order
replacing the word 'half' with 'quarter'.

Devoted, still, to his doomed cause
the Captain grabbed a splintered oar,
and cried: 'Come back then! One more round!
We'll see just *who* is going down!'

At which there was a chilling rumble,
which caused the last few crew to tumble
into the waves (which claimed their lives).
I braced myself for *my* demise,

as Sea Snail surged from lowest reaches
and dashed the *Treader* into pieces.
She struck the ship again, again,
till only splinters did remain.

I floundered in the crashing surf,
but vaguely managed to observe
the Great Green Sea Snail's head, receded,
regretful that this act was needed.

I saw her blink, shake off the woe,
prepare herself to dive below –
until she spotted one survivor,
and so (with all that spare saliva)

the Sea Snail swiftly doubled back
and had herself a post-war snack;
she didn't leave a lone spectator,
she swallowed Max (and your narrator).

On waking up inside the snail
I feared that we might not prevail;
as science now claims, uncontested,
the belly's where things get digested.

But lying there, Max reconsidered
the course that led him to these innards,
and spoke (at last) of his beginning,
of days when fortune still was with him.

When Max was Phil, and young, he spent
his days at large in rural Kent;
before his mind had time to harden,
he lived his life out in the garden.

His parents were organic folk,
but sadly, young Phil's heart was broke
when they both died from driving, drinking
(*not* from snails, as I was thinking).

With no relations, Phil left pretty
rural Kent for life mid-city;
assigned to live with other waifs
in council buildings, low on space.

But Phil refused to quit just yet,
the rules he chose to circumvent –
he saved his pennies, bought some seeds,
and filled his room with bright green leaves.

One day, there came some thrilling news:
a family who, when asked to choose
a child from his home's vast supply,
had (just this once) not passed him by.

He spent the week before their meeting
pruning, watering and weeding
(and kept his window open wide
to let some half-fresh air inside).

He met the couple in the lobby,
conversed about his favourite hobby,
invited them to see his room;
his great creations, out in bloom.

(By now engrossed, I held my breath
suspecting what would happen next;
that what the couple went to see
meant Max might have it in for me.)

Sure enough, behind the door
was Phil's formation, bright no more.
A sight straight from a horror scene –
it seemed a gang of *snails* had been.

Poor Phil could not explain his loss.
The family promptly brushed him off,
and he grew up leaf-free, alone;
convinced snail-kind had stole his home.

In later years, he turned his rage
to help design a product range;
he named his company PEST KILL MAX
and changed his name to match the packs.

'And so,' Max finished, 'understand
just why it was I always planned
at journey's end to squash *you* flat –
but now I can't do even that.'

(The positions we held in the tube
did not allow his legs to move;
all Max could do was softly cry
and wish all mollusc-kind would die.)

That's tragic, came a sudden voice
(though Max did not hear any noise.
I guessed, since I alone heard speech,
our host spoke through telepathy).

*Yes... Hi! I'm sorry 'bout this greeting
so soon after you both got eaten.
But snail, please ask... I'd like it solved,
just how I came to be involved.*

'But... I can't speak!' I said. Aloud.
Poor Max's eyes popped halfway out.
*I have the power to grant you speech,
now ask him why he hunted ME!*

'She says, er... Why did you pursue
the Great Green Sea Snail's trail of glue?
I mean, come on, you can't believe
that it was *her* who ate your leaves...'

Max, shocked by this sudden query,
replied with answer and a theory:
'It just seemed like the thing to do!
The Sea Snail's speaking using you?'

'The good is what you're angry at,'
I said. 'And yeah, Great Green said that.'
Max spoke again: 'I want her dead,
because she's snail-kind's figurehead!'

'Her race, who chewed my childhood leaves,
left ship and crewmen, lost at sea,
to drown beneath the salty swell.
And now she's eaten me as well!'

Oh Max, she answered, *all must eat.*
But unlike you, the only meat
that I particularly devour
is that of the sea-cauliflower.

Snails eat plants, it's what we do!
It doesn't mean we're after you,
the flora in young Phil's display
helped some young snail live one more day.

'Wait a sec!' I said. 'Hang on.
Max – can I ask just how long
you left the room, that fateful night
you say the snail-gang ruined your life?'

'Er... fifteen minutes, tops.' He frowned,
and more so when I gasped, aloud.
Soon Sea Snail made the same deduction:
You smart oesophageal obstruction!

'It takes us hours to move one metre!
It's our most famed, distinctive feature!
Don't you see just what this means?
It *wasn't us* who ate your dreams!'

Max's mouth fell open wide.
His eyes stared at the Snail's insides,
but focused somewhere far beyond –
the past. Young Phil had got it wrong.

As Max let out a single tear,
Great Green chipped in: *You're no use here.*
Take notice of my cousin's point –
go treat us well! Don't disappoint!

And then, as sudden as we came
inside the Snail, we left again
(though I would hesitate to guess
which orifice released her guests).

SIX: JOLLY OLD SAINT PHIL (FORMERLY MAX)

Though cast once more into the waves
both man and snail were quickly saved –
I used my newfound 'magic throat'
to hail a passing fishing boat.

We didn't speak much, sailing back.
This was a new, more thoughtful Max;
and though I'd kept the power of speech
no apt remarks occurred to me.

(Plus, if I was overheard,
the sailors may have been disturbed;
I wanted all their concentration
fixed on tasks of navigation.)

Once safely back upon the shore
it seemed clear Max had been reformed;
he set me free, and made it plain
he'd never harm a snail again

(but plotted vengeance on the head
of the boy that family picked instead,
whose hands – now Phil brought him to mind –
were oddly *green* to wave goodbye).

No sooner than he'd said 'hello'
he bought his wife a new crossbow;
and on some sunset-smothered hill
he whispered to her: 'Call me Phil'...

and filled with newfound glee, next day,
they bought a house out rural way,
with a garden you might call 'exquisite';
in part fenced off, so snails could visit.

And me? My talent did not fade,
in fact, I learnt to conversate
more than you lot with each other;
though mostly I choose not to bother.

Except... to stop the world forgetting,
I do a turn at fêtes and weddings;
telling guests this haunting story
of Max, and his mad quest for glory,

of how the Sea Snail changed his mind,
of how our mollusc brains (combined)
restored the sense to hateful Max
by just restating simple facts;

of how the sailor ceased to quarrel
when life revealed this simple moral:
'He prayeth well who loveth well
both man and bird and beast... and *snail*.'

A Shell of My Former Self

or, 'Snail Moves On'

You're probably wondering if we pass it on
in the manner of car, or house –
the answer is both. Also, like clothes.

So: 'detached, one careful owner,
size sixteen.' I had a lovely lady
hermit crab round yesterday,
looking to downsize for retirement.
'The kids have all grown up, moved out,'
she said, though she wasn't married.
I don't judge. I showed her the spiral staircase,
the games room, upstairs loo;
let her know I'd a family of woodlice
coming round later. Asked if she liked lettuce
at all, by way of conversation. You must
make an effort – plus, I was nervous.
It's like showing someone round your soul,
or a part of your body... that one
particularly.

        But it *is* strange. This is the place
I used to retreat to, when I needed
to feel safe – where I could really
be myself, you know? Contents just so,
everything perfect. Hard to let go. Anyway,
she told me she's more into seaweed.

Her offer wasn't quite what I wanted.
I've been eyeing up a yellow number
two houses along... nice bit of moss
round the doorway, like something
from childhood. Currently used

for decorative purposes, I assume. Sits
in a flower bed, and I've not seen it move.
Yes, I'll be happy there, once I shift
this old weight from my back,
once I clear out the attic. And yet –
my shell has been good to me;
seen me through all weathers,
no trouble from predators,
my choice of neighbours.
And when I curled up at night
inside, I knew I was home...

                              Oh,

I'm fine. This is just me, droning on,
when I'm sure you have somewhere to go.

But if you're ever in need of a paperweight,
or an interesting ornament –
let me know.

A Snail of Two Cities

'It was the best of times...
... it is a far, far better rest I go to.'

From Liverpool to Londonderry
I 'barnacled' it on the ferry.

From Newcastle to Whitley Bay
I hid amidst a large toupée.

From Bath to Weston-Super-Mare
I clutched a shoe to get me there.

From Middlesbrough to Holyhead
I rode as keepsake, playing dead.

One day I'll die for real, they say.
'Snails weren't meant to live this way!'

But I explain I'm well prepared
for the day my life cannot be spared,

as on the day we don't recover
we move from one place to another –

for, as times go, I've had the best,
to be only bettered by the rest.

Gandhi's Snail

Pacifist? Aggression-less,
non-violent protest?
We got all that covered.
You heard it here first –

Mahatma G. grew up
a true teenage rebel,
till he met his first snail
and his views were reversed.

Snail's Sense of Self

National Poetry Day, 2010. Official theme: Home.
Official symbol: a Snail.

Home? I myself am home,
either way I turn is home.
Anywhere I lay my head.

I am under no illusions.
I am not the jaguar,
no tiger, burning bright;
not the fuzzy squirrel,
not the cruel black crow.
In the ring-fight of the animals
I would be among the first to go.

I am not a good mascot,
certainly no fashion statement.
Can't do a day's honest graft.
I won't keep the rats at bay,
or the flies. Can't fetch a stick,
or lead the blind. My song,
on tape, will not relax you;
I have no star sign.

I inspire no cartoon antics,
no-one wants me for their pet;
try, and you will fail
to have a snail
seen at the vet.

I am no lovesick swan, or penguin,
I barely even have a sex.

But there must be a place for me,
o traveller of the pavements,

of the hedgerows, over nations –
although it takes a while –
a place for one who'll happily pack
his troubles up, and smile.

I *am* the stuff of poetry.
We all are, in the end.
Just keep me in your heart,
your works of art,
I'll be your friend.

A Snail's Pace

Slower than the motion
of an oceanic plate.
Confucius says: 'Man who employs snail
must learn to wait' –

must learn to put away his watch,
and find a different pace.

Your man must learn
this life which we are leading
is no race –

for snail has much to teach him,
before man can be great.

Snail's Postcard from Heaven

You'll be flicking through your 'snail mail',
and wondering who this postcard's from –
the blank, no-name-been-given one...

so let me tell you. Yes, it's me,
the snail that you once stood on.

And the postcard isn't blank, it's just
the God of Snails' almighty light,
screwing with the contrast.

Anyway – how are you doing?
From my new celestial slithering grounds
(where lettuce comprises each surface)
I've kept a watchful eye on you
to see if my message sunk in.

And what did I see, on peering down?
You, churning out snail poetry.
Whether from guilt, or inspiration –
I don't know. But God got me a copy.

And frankly, I'm impressed!
You wrote me quite a handsome legacy.
It seems I've managed more by death
(and haunting) than Mum dreamed for me.

So now? I'm just relaxing, mostly.
Reading through your verse, quite happy,
having a snail of a time. Except,
I feel the book needs one more thing:
I've spotted an omission.

So I thought I'd send this postcard,
for inclusion in the next edition.

I'm having far more fun up here
than I could if I was living,
so rest your pen, J.M. And yes –
my friend, *you are forgiven.*

THE EMMA PRESS

small press, big dreams

The Emma Press is an independent publisher dedicated to producing books which are sweet, funny and beautiful. It was founded in 2012 in Winnersh, UK, by Emma Wright and the first Emma Press book, *The Flower and the Plough* by Rachel Piercey, was published in January 2013.

Our current publishing programme includes a mixture of themed poetry anthologies and single-author pamphlets, with an ongoing engagement with the works of the Roman poet Ovid. We publish poems and books which excite us, and we are often on the lookout for new writing.

Visit our website and sign up to the Emma Press newsletter to hear about all upcoming calls for submissions as well as our events and publications. You can also purchase our other titles and poetry-related stationery in our online shop.

http://theemmapress.com

Also from The Emma Press:

The Emma Press Anthology of Mildly Erotic Verse — ISBN: 978 0 9574596 2 5 — Price: £10 / $17

A beautiful anthology which celebrates modern eroticism in all its messy, sexy glory.

A Poetic Primer for Love and Seduction
ISBN: 978 0 9574596 3 2 — Price: £10 / $17

Romantic adventurers! Look no further for your new handbook, full of advice in matters of the heart and boudoir.

The Emma Press Anthology of Motherhood
ISBN: 978 0 9574596 7 0 — Price: £10 / $17

Love and devotion sit alongside exhaustion and doubt in this moving collection about mothers and motherhood.

The Emma Press Anthology of Fatherhood
ISBN: 978 1 910139 00 4 — Price: £10 / $17

A deeply affecting collection which explores themes of joy, masculinity, expectations, disappointment and deep love.

Homesickness and Exile (Sept 2014)
ISBN: 978 1 910139 02 8 — Price: £10 / $17

A collection of poems about longing and belonging, and about chosen homes, rootlessness, and emotional and physical exile.

Best Friends Forever (Dec 2014)
ISBN: 978 1 910139 07 3 — Price: £10 / $17

A celebration of this frequently-overlooked relationship: the intimate and the casual, the life sustaining and the life changing.

Captain Love and the Five Joaquins
by John Clegg
ISBN: 978 1 910139 01 1 — Price: £5 / $9

Clegg thrills and intrigues with this true adventure story, set in the Old West and told through verse and prose poems.

The Held and the Lost
by Kristen Roberts
ISBN: 978 0 9574596 8 7 — Price: £5 / $9

A moving collection of distinctly Australian poems about love, marriage and family life.

The Emmores
by Richard O'Brien
ISBN: 978 0 9574596 4 9 — Price: £5 / $9

An irresistible mix of tender odes, introspective sonnets, exuberant free verse and anthems of sexual persuasion.

The Flower and the Plough,
by Rachel Piercey
ISBN: 978 0 9574596 0 1 — Price: £5 / $9

A nuanced study of passion and heartbreak which captures the extravagant surrender of early love to the raw ache.

Raspberries for the Ferry
by Andrew Wynn Owen
ISBN: 978 0 9574596 5 6 — Price: £6.50 / $12

Tortoises, dancers, lovers and whales all beguile in this treasury of gorgeous, tart, juicy poems.

Ikhda, by Ikhda
by Ikhda Ayuning Maharsi
ISBN: 978 0 9574596 6 3 — Price: £6.50 / $12

Reading this book is like being splashed with freezing water and showered with popping candy and wild roses.